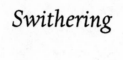

Swithering

by the same author

A PAINTED FIELD

SLOW AIR

ROBIN ROBERTSON

Swithering

A HARVEST ORIGINAL

HARCOURT, INC.

Orlando ★ *Austin* ★ *New York* ★ *San Diego* ★ *Toronto* ★ *London*

Requests for permission to make copies of any part
of the work should be mailed to the following address:
Permissions Department, Harcourt, Inc.,
6277 Sea Harbor Drive, Orlando, Florida 32887-6777.

www.HarcourtBooks.com
First published in the United Kingdom by Picador.

Library of Congress Cataloging-in-Publication Data
Robertson, Robin, 1955-
Swithering / Robin Robertson.– 1st U.S. ed.
p. cm.
"A Harvest original."
I. Title.
PR6068.O1925S95 2006
821'.914—dc22   2005026176
ISBN-13: 978-0-15-603199-8 ISBN-10: 0-15-603199-X

Text set in Dante
Designed by April Ward

Printed in the United States of America
First U.S. edition
A C E G I H F D B

for my brother
Tim Robertson

The flowers of the forest they ask it of me,
How many strawberries grow in the salt sea?
And I answered to them with a tear in my eye,
How many dark ships sail the forest?

'The False Bride'

I've been down to the greenwood;
Mother, mak my bed soon,
For I'm weary o' hunting,
And fain would lie doon

'Lord Randal'

I was climbing to a tree that was too high for me,
Asking fruit where there weren't any grew;
I been lifting warm water out aneath cold clay,
And against the streams I was rowing

But I mean to climb up some higher higher tree,
To harry a white snowflake's nest,
And down shall I fall, ay, without any fear,
To the arms that love me the best

'False, False'

CONTENTS

I

The Park Drunk 3

Trysts 4

At Dawn 5

What the Horses See at Night 6

Primavera 8

Cusp 9

The Eel 10

The Death of Actaeon 12

Swimming in the Woods 18

Drowning in Co. Down 19

Ghost of a Garden 20

Selkie 21

Between the Harvest
and the Hunter's Moon 22

Old Ways 25

Entry 26

Samhain 27

Still Life with
Cardoon and Carrots 28

Strindberg in London 29

Wormwood 30

The Glair 31

Strindberg in Paris 32

Heel of Bread 33

Entropy 34

Sea-Fret 35

Myth 40

II

New York Spring *43*

The Lake at Dusk *44*

A Seagull Murmur *46*

Calcutta, Co. Armagh *47*

Mar-Hawk *48*

The Catch *49*

Actaeon: the Early Years *50*

To My Daughters, Asleep *55*

Firesetting *56*

Siesta *57*

La Stanza delle Mosche 58

Lizard 59

Ode to Conger-Eel Broth 60

Asparagus 63

On Pharos 64

Manifest 65

Untitled (51) 66

Net 68

Crossing the Archipelago 70

Bow 71

Rainmaker 72

The Custom-House 73

Leavings 74

Donegal 75

Trumpeter Swan 76

Answers 77

Holding Proteus 78

notes and acknowledgements 81

Swithering

I

THE PARK DRUNK

He opens his eyes to a hard frost,
the morning's soft amnesia of snow.

The thorned stems of gorse
are starred crystal; each bud
like a candied fruit, its yellow
picked out and lit
by the low pulse
of blood-orange
riding in the eastern trees.

What the snow has furred
to silence, uniformity,
frost amplifies, makes singular:
giving every form a sound,
an edge, as if
frost wants to know what
snow tries to forget.

And so he drinks for winter,
for the coming year,
to open all the beautiful tiny doors
in their craquelure of frost;
and he drinks
like the snow falling, trying
to close the biggest door of all.

TRYSTS

meet me
where the sun goes down
meet me
in the cave, under the battleground
meet me
on the broken branch
meet me
in the shade, below the avalanche
meet me
under the witch's spell
meet me
tonight, in the wishing well
meet me
on the famine lawn
meet me
in the eye of the firestorm
meet me
in your best shoes
and your favourite dress
meet me
on your own, in the wilderness
meet me
as my lover, as my only friend
meet me
on the river bed

AT DAWN

I took a new path off the mountain
to this ruined croft, and went inside
to find, under the trestle table,
the earth floor seething with ants;
on the mantelpiece,
some wire-wool, a box of screws,
a biscuit-tin of human hair
and a urine sample
with my name and date of birth.
In each corner, something else:
five blackthorn pins beside
five elder twigs, freshly cut
and red at both ends, tied up
with ribbons into the shape of a man;
the blade-bone of a sheep;
a mackerel
wrapped in today's paper, one eye
looking up at me
through its greased window;
the lopped head of a roe deer,
its throat full of wire.
The last thing I found
was a photograph of me,
looking slightly younger,
stretched out, on a trestle table.

WHAT THE HORSES SEE AT NIGHT

When the day-birds have settled
in their creaking trees,
the doors of the forest open
for the flitting
drift of deer
among the bright croziers
of new ferns
and the legible stars;
foxes stream from the earth;
a tawny owl
sweeps the long meadow.
In a slink of river-light,
the mink's face
is already slippery with yolk,
and the bay's
tiny islands are drops
of solder
under a drogue moon.
The sea's a heavy sleeper,
dreaming in and out with a catch
in each breath, and is not disturbed
by that *plowt*—the first
in a play of herring, a shoal
silvering open
the sheeted black skin of the sea.
Through the starting rain, the moon
skirrs across the sky dragging
torn shreds of cloud behind.

The fox's call is red
and ribboned
in the snow's white shadow.
The horses watch the sea climb
and climb and walk
towards them on the hill,
hear the vole
crying under the alder,
our children
breathing slowly in their beds.

PRIMAVERA

for Cait

The brimstone is back
in the woken hills of Vallombrosa,
passing the word
from speedwell to violet
wood anemone to celandine.
I could walk to you now
with Spring just ahead of me,
north over flat ground
at two miles an hour,
the sap moving with me,
under the rising
grass of the field
like a dragged magnet,
the lights of the flowers
coming on in waves
as I walked with the budburst
and the flushing of trees.
If I started now,
I could bring you the Spring
for your birthday.

CUSP

The child's skip
still there in the walk,
a woman's poise in her slow
examination
of the brightly coloured globe, this
toy of the world.
Is there anything
more heartbreaking than hope?

THE EEL

after Montale

The eel, siren
of the coldest seas, leaves behind the Baltic
for our warmer waters,
reaching our estuaries, our rivers,
and lancing upstream hard against the current
from branch to branch,
vein to vein, narrowing
ever inward, ever deeper
into the heart of the sandstone,
threading the thick, channelling mud until
—one morning—a dart of light, loosed
through the chestnut trees,
ignites her glimmer, her muscle,
there in the dead pools
in the pleated grooves that stream the sides
of the Apennines down to Romagna;
the eel: firebrand, whiplash, shot
bolt of the earth's desire,
aimed, by these dried-up gullies and river-beds,
at the dark paradise of her spawning;
she is the green spirit looking for life
in the tight jaw of drought and desolation,
she is the spark which says
that all begins where all appears to end,
here, with this charred, half-buried stick;
the quick rainbow

a twin to your own bright eyes:
shining out
among a generation mired in mud—
can you not see
that she is your sister?

THE DEATH OF ACTAEON

after Ovid

for James Lasdun

Noon: midsummer; Mount Cithaeron.
The baking ground is brown with the blood of beasts, drained
since dawn by Actaeon and his men; their nets
are stiff with it. It cakes their hands, their spear-shafts.
Enough for one day, they head for shade to dream of water.

      ★

There was a deep cleft in the mountain, meshed
with cypresses and pine; in it, a distant
speck of glass: the sacred pool.
Hot from the hunt, the huntress-queen
would come to this grove
to cool herself in the pure water:
daughter of Zeus, twin sister of Apollo, protectress
of these wild woods and these mountains:
the virgin goddess, Artemis.

Twenty Amnisian nymphs attend their queen.
As she steps into the pool, they stand aside
while the deftest folds the locks of hair into a knot.
Scooping a palmful of water to her neck and throat,
letting it run the length of her, she straightens in the sunlight,
her back's curve bending like a longbow
as she raises her arms to unbind the knot,
shake loose her hair
and stretch.

Arms outspread,
one step at a time,
he inched down
through the cooling air,
to enter
—though he did not know it—
the grove of Artemis.
He parted the branches,
slipping through ferns
that dripped with spray,
and reached the grassy bank
and the murmur of voices, or water.
Edging into the open,
he saw stillness
and grace, in the space of one heartbeat;
then he saw his own death.

Like gazelles at a waterhole sensing a lion,
the handmaidens turned their heads
and the glass split.
Light went everywhere
—into the screams as they covered their breasts,
into the water, as they thrashed it white,
crowding round their goddess, trying
to hide her body with their own.
But she stood too high above them, and began to burn—
and turned away, glaring over her shoulder,
as if to reach for an arrow
from a quiver that wasn't there.
There was no weapon but water.
Enraged, she caught up a handful
and flung it in his face,

leaving a trail of gold as she spoke these words:
'Now go and tell, if you can,
that you have seen the goddess Artemis naked.'

With that, a rack of branching stag horns
burst from his wet brow.
Actaeon felt his bones stretch and the sinews snap
as she lengthened his neck, drew the tips of his ears to a point,
put hooves in place of hands and feet,
turned his arms into forelegs that reached and lunged
as his hindlegs tensed and gathered,
and thickened his pale skin to a brindled hide.
And last of all she poured a white fear into his heart
like a stream of other blood. And it was done.

He fled.
Sharp hooves bit into the ground,
horns clattering the branches—
plunging out across the grove in springs and bounds
he was amazed by his own lightness.
But when he saw his antlered head
looking back at him from a mountain pool, he knew
only his mind remained—and it was scattered—
torn between running home to the palace,
or hiding out here in the woods; torn between shame and fear.

As he hesitated, the dogs caught his trail
and decided for him: first to give tongue were Blackclaw
and keen-scented Tracer, never mistaken:
Tracer a Cretan dog, Blackclaw a Spartan; then others
came rushing on, wave on successive wave:
Stag-chaser, Ravener, Fell-ranger—all from Arcadia—
Fawnbane the fawn-killer, Hurricane and Death-bringer,

Wingfeet, the swift of foot, Hunter the hungry,
the boar-scarred Sylvan, Harrier the wolf-dog,
Shepherd the rallier; Grappler with her black kin,
Catcher from Sicyon, thin in the flank; Runner and Courser,
Blazon and Tiger, the roistering Ravager,
white-coated Frost-biter and black-haired Mourner,
and fast at their shoulders, famed for his strength, came Spartan,
and Tempest, renowned for his stamina,
Wildfire and Wolf-taker with her brother The Cyprian,
Grasper with his white star, Bristler and Blackbeard,
Lightfoot and White-tooth, shrill-tongued Ring-the-Wood,
And others, many others, it would take too long to name.

Locked on to their quarry,
the whole pack, thick with bloodlust,
flowed over the rocks and crags, over the trackless cliffs
—where the way is hard, or where there is no way at all.
He leapt and jinked through the killing grounds
longing to cry out: 'I am Actaeon!
Don't you know your own master?' but there was no sound
but the baying of dogs; the air cracked with their barking.
And then they came.
The three out-runners spilled through the trees to outstrip
    the others.
Hellhound clamped his teeth—with two puffs of red—
into his master's back, then Deerkiller and Hill-Fury
latched to his shoulder and hung on.

While they held down their prey,
the rest of the pack broke on him like surf,
dipping their teeth into his flesh
till there was no place left for further wounds,
and at every wound's mouth was the mouth of a dog.

Surge upon surge, the riptide crashed and turned,
battening on, and tearing away—maddened—in the red spume.
Actaeon groaned: a sound which wasn't human,
but which no stag could produce.
Falling to his knees, like a supplicant at prayer, he bowed
in silence as the angry sea crashed on him once again
and the dogs hid his body with their own.
Drowning now,
his horned head reared, streaming, from the ruck,
as if a god was being born
—not a mortal soul transformed and torn apart.
The huntsmen looked around for Actaeon: calling
—each louder than the one before—for Actaeon,
as if he weren't there.
Should he not share this unexpected gift?
This sixteen-pointer brought to bay?
Actaeon turned his head at the sound of his name.
He wished he were as far away as they thought;
or watching this death, not living it.
And his dogs kept swivelling round to look for their master,
barking their signal for him to come,
come and dispatch the beast they'd brought down;
and Actaeon turned again.
Then for the last time
the thirsty hounds surrounded him,
closed over him,
worked their heads into his body,
and tore him, inside out.
Then, and only then, they say,
was the anger of Artemis, goddess of chastity, appeased.

*

It is also said that the dogs devoured the body, then hunted for Actaeon in vain throughout the forest. Finally their search brought them to the cave of Chiron the centaur, who had fostered Actaeon as a child and taught him how to hunt. Only after he had fashioned a statue of their lost master could the dogs be calmed and allow themselves to be led home.

SWIMMING IN THE WOODS

Her long body in the spangled shade of the wood
was a swimmer moving through a pool:
fractal, finned by leaf and light;
the loose plates of lozenge and rhombus
wobbling coins of sunlight.
When she stopped, the water stopped,
and the sun re-made her as a tree,
banded and freckled and foxed.

Besieged by symmetries, condemned
to these patterns of love and loss,
I stare at the wet shape on the tiles
till it fades; when she came and sat next to me
after her swim and walked away
back to the trees, she left a dark butterfly.

DROWNING IN CO. DOWN

This place can't hold enough rain.
The land rots houses just to
get them out of the way, get closer
to the heavy sky.
People drink all day if they can,
the water-table their only gravity.

If they drift away they come back
thirsty, missing the pints, that
loose decay of light;
scuttling their ships
in the usual harbours, growing old
watching the water rise,

their options narrowing
to this country town,
this bar, these optics,
a whiskey glass,
the softened mouth
of this swollen ground.

GHOST OF A GARDEN

Sometimes I discover I have gone downstairs,
crossed the grass and found myself
in here: the tool-shed,
caught in a lash of brambles, bindweed
and tall ivied trees like pipecleaners. It looks out,
vacantly, on a garden run to seed:
the lost tennis court, grown-over benches,
a sunken barbecue snagged with blown roses.
The courtyard walls are full of holes the swallows
try to sew, in and out of them like open doors.
In the corner of the shed my father is weeping
and I cannot help him because he is dead.

SELKIE

in memory of Michael Donaghy

'I'm not stopping,'
he said, shrugging off his skin
like a wet-suit, then stretching it
on the bodhrán's frame,
'let's play.'
And he played till dawn:
all the jigs and reels
he knew, before he stood
and drained the last
from his glass, slipped back in
to the seal-skin,
into a new day, saluting us
with that famous grin:
'That's me away.'

BETWEEN THE HARVEST
AND THE HUNTER'S MOON

Returning from war, or the rumours of war,
I shelter in the lee of the great stone eagle's head
that marks the edge of Carn Boel,
what remains of my uniform
tattered and tailed
as velvet from antlers, as moss
flayed from this stretching rack of rock.

From here, the sea is scalloped
in marbled endpapers of green and blue and grey;
it's hard to tell if the long black shapes
are drifting seals, or reefs,
or sailors sleeping in the shallows.
Waves trail in, darkening with height and depth,
almost black before they turn
and crush themselves white:
the rocks milking the wave to a froth of sea-foam
blown two hundred feet up
onto this cliff-edge
to join the bog cotton.
The sea hollows out dolmens,
chambered cairns and standing stones
in the slow worship of erosion.

Under the still October sun
the stones are dancing in the fields,
bright-diademed with lichen;
the sea below begins to slide and pitch, the sun
shattering again and again
to a million answering lights.

From the Armed Knight to Nanjizal,
the rain's grey searchlights
draw across the headlands,
flushing out the birds: the wheedling
keck of jackdaws, as they throw themselves
like soot around the deep ravine;
crows and bald-faced rooks
make heavy weather of the tussock grass;
the raven croaks its thick call
as it levers itself into the air:
a deep and hollow *pruk pruk pruk*.
Above them, through the ribs of rain,
triangulating gulls monitor the turn in the day,
inclining into the gale's brunt, the coming storm.

Grass struggles in its thin veneer of earth,
among this embattled work of stone: granite
crenellated by wind, imbedded with feldspar,
mica, quartz, and the thin black
crystal threads of tourmaline.
I carry stones wherever I go:
it is bad luck not to leave
a cairn on top of the rock,
a stone on top of the cairn.
I shoulder my pack and walk on.

The land is draining of colour and life:
the hills russet and grey
with spent bracken and heather.
Wind ploughs the moor-grass
along the grain of sheep-runs;
the sheep huddle at the wind's mouth
with the first lash of rain, the scour,

stripping the sycamores of their last leaves,
the torrent leashing down.
Thrushes and blackbirds
flit through driven wind; the larks
frantic in the blackthorn,
in the lanterns of gorse, and all this
lit by a wrecking light.

Darkness comes down
like an empty glass
and the ground shakes off the last of the rain.
I reach the elm-wood,
under the rookery,
slip a bullet in the breech and wait here
in this dark,
between the harvest and the hunter's moon.

OLD WAYS

We are near to the place
where they make the leather ghosts:
shoulder-bags like lost children,
purses shaped as cloven hooves
so you can walk to the shops
holding the devil's hand.

ENTRY

A buzzard works the fields
behind the harvesting:
the slung bolt of her body
balanced in the wind
by wings and tail, hanging
over the machine blades
and the soft flesh far below
—a rabbit
exposed in the shorn stalks—
and she's holding,
holds still
till her wings fall away and she drops
like a slate into snow.
The wounds feather through him
throwing a fine mist of incarnation,
annunciation in the fletched field,
and she breaks in,
flips the latches
of the back, opens the red drawer
in his chest, ransacking the heart.

SAMHAIN

My daughters, playing at witch and devil, gaze
at our visitor, lantern-jawed
in his orange and black; they stare at him,
at the liver-spots on his empty hands.

By the light of the long-fires, the soft
mouth of the turnip-lantern curls in,
blue-white and pursed, a candy-floss
of mould around the chin.

A guest is as good as a ghost at this time,
at the hinge of the year when the gap
between the shades and the shadowed is just
slow air. Our last apples stale in his lap.

STILL LIFE WITH CARDOON AND CARROTS

Juan Sánchez Cotán, 1603, oil on canvas

These are not the instruments of Christ's Passion
spotlit in the frame of the niche: not nails
but carrots, not the flail of the Flagellation
but a cardoon. And this is not an altar, or an altarpiece
but a *cantarero*: a Toledan larder. Here
is the beginning of Spanish still-life.

Cardoon, from the Latin *cardus*: an artichoke,
whose thorny thistle-head was used for carding wool;
a winter vegetable with ridged stalks like celery,
but wide and white, curving like ribs from the root.
Sánchez Cotán would have eaten them, blanched,
in salads, or cooked them, with the carrots, in a stew.

Thirty years later, Zurbarán would complete the picture,
and provide the lamb: filling the same black larder
with his own bound and sorrowful *Agnus Dei*.

STRINDBERG IN LONDON

My new wife fills the bed, fills every room, tells me
it will all be fine. Dragged through other people's lives,
pursued through my own. What will I remember?
Only this. Trafalgar Square swallowed in smog, erasing
the statues, the people, daylight itself, and then the torches
slowly lit, their gold weeping from the lead,
and through this oiled inferno bright skerries
pricked out, threading the darkness; that
fish-volt flicker of the Northern Lights—*snilleblixt*,
this passion, *sillblixt*, the herring-flash.

WORMWOOD

for Don Paterson

A flight of loose stairs off the street into a high succession
of empty rooms, prolapsed chairs and a memory of women
perfumed with hand-oil and *artemisia absinthium*:
wormwood to me, and to the sappy Russian sailors, *chernobyl*.
The scooped-back ballroom gown
shows the tell-tale bra-strap, red and tired.
'Leave it,' my maths master used to say at a dropped pencil,
'it can't fall any further.' Well, I couldn't, and neither could she.

THE GLAIR

The slow drag across the sandpaper,
scratching smoke
from the head of the match
again and again until it flares.
Lamplight lies heavy on her breasts,
her flanks; the hand's passage
slow as ceremony, persistent
as a dream unsleeved; the spark
drawn in hard with a catch
of flame: the lumbering storm
and the white bolt, the bright rope, on
and on and on. The albumen. The glair.

STRINDBERG IN PARIS

In his single room in the Latin Quarter,
stripped to the waist, hunched
over the crucible, his sulphur's
halting flame, the crippled Firegod
forging lines of gold from lead.
A gift for his lost wife and children,
this was to be the Great Work:
a golden net invisible to the eye
and finer than spider-thread.
With every word he wrote, his hands bled.

HEEL OF BREAD

The spatter of rain
at the window

sounds
like crackling flames;

the writhe and twist
as you

slit yourself on me,
riding my hand.

Rain
flails against the glass.

I have made
a litter of my life.

No news, no
new descent:

It's over, you said,
this is the last time.

I consider
the wine-stains,

the obligatory
heel of bread.

ENTROPY

Not praying, just shielding my eyes from the glare
of streets, the city's free-for-all: crowds
in Brownian motion, eight million magnets
repulsing or attracting, hackled like attack dogs
or hot-wired to this smear of light and speed,
gunning the gas. An emulsion of longing, a brawling
bright cacophony of dreck.
The colour-wheel spins to white.
Police tapes whip and gutter in the wind
like catching fire; dust-devils corkscrew litter
under concrete halls, into slack canals
prismatic with oil. The city saw my hesitation-marks,
found my seam, and ripped. Night flails
with sirens, the street-lamp's sodium
bars the back wall. I close my eyes;
not praying, just on my knees in the dark.

SEA-FRET

(Tynemouth Priory)

The North Light gone
in a smoke of sea-spray,
its stone still riding in
and out of sight; the frayed
pennons and bannerets
of the tide-crests
all that is visible now,
in the haar-light
and the shoaling rain.
The sea moves its white hands
along the breakwater, blindly
trying for a way in;
percussive waves
crash and recoil
at the base of the cliff,
slow and attritional
under the east salient,
scathing the stone revetment
with that interminable refrain,
that petitionary, leaden
litany of the sea.

Kittiwakes quarter
the grey sweep, mewling
through a squall of sea-wired
black-backed gulls.
Oblivious,
stunt-flying fulmars

stall and glide, sail-
planing in long curves,
letting their feet
drag each brake and turn
as they skim the sides
of Penbal Crag—the head
of the rampart on the rock.

*

Where broken and eroded stones
still reef the headland's brow,
the burial-ground's strewn markers
paraphrase—in simple miniature—
the fretted ruin
of the thousand-year-old priory:
these worn gravestones, sea-dimpled,
honeycombed by salt.

*

The chantry's rose-window
sights east along the barrel
of the rusted 6-inch gun.
By the remains of the lighthouse
and the battery observation post,
the Benedictine well:
the cover of the well
the iris shutter,
the well-water its lens.
The unchanging view
from this camera obscura
never the same:
the colours
of the northern sky,

each day's
dispersion
to a glossary of light.

            *

A face of steel and concrete
on a head of stone,
the gun emplacements
stare out narrowly
at the open sea.
Underneath, under ground,
soft workers of the inner body
move in its dark cloister,
candled here and there
by lamps in glazed recesses
set in the passage wall.
Shell canisters gleam
bluntly in the claustral light,
stacked on wooden skidding racks,
un-armed as yet, unblessed.

At the copper door
of the shifting lobby
—the sacristy or tiring-house—
the rubric demands the ritual:
Wipe your boots and shoes
on Mat 'B'; remove
your outer garments
and hang them on Peg 'A'.
Pass the barrier in your socks
and underclothes, put on
the magazine clothes 'C'

and magazine shoes 'D'
and go to your work.

In linen vestments and felt slippers
the working-party
enters the cartridge store.
Behind them, on hooks,
their accoutrements and uniform,
boots lined up, bright
along the darkened floor.
The metal buttons glint; the polished
steel-caps
flint and spark.

Inside the shell-filling room, the solemn
and most tender rite of ordinance:
the raising of the shell to the shell-block;
the slotting-home of the cartridge;
the slow
elevation of the charged shell.
The platen is wiped clean of powder
and the process begins again.

A bell is rung in the sealed chamber:
the transfigured steel
is drawn above
and issued to the guns.

                ★

The wind off the sea
like a thrown knife;
a styptic cold
over the concrete half-moon batteries,

the barbican and sanctuary:
all the exposed relics
in this reliquary of light.

There is no raised stone
the rain cannot macerate.
Rust, the penetrant,
turns iron maculate:
leaving it,
flaked to a filigree of red.
The edging wind eats everything.

Under the crucial rock,
alexanders and brassica
are all that remain
of the monks' garden:
Mediterranean imports
gone native
into the saxifrage and sea-fern grass,
the thrift and red valerian.

The scrub peters out
as the land falls away, into cliff,
as it all falls away
into sea air.
The waves reducing
all this handiwork to a shell,
and all the shells to sand.

MYTH

This morning, in bracken
beyond the east field,
I find the blown bulbs of sunset;
on the wet lawn,
after the snow,
the snowman's spine.

II

NEW YORK SPRING

Couples strolling
through stopped light,
the cherry's slew of blossom, those
fallen shells of pink magnolia,
the inconsolable sadness of this
Saturday in Central Park.

The trail gone
under the blossom and I think
of all my loves and how I lost them,
walking the only path
allowed to me
from all the roads I chose.

Beyond the lake
an accordion's slow polka, its broken
soundtrack foundering,
stopping, starting over;
the girls have all gone home now,
I know, I don't need to be told.
The dance finished
twenty years ago.

THE LAKE AT DUSK

I watch the day break down
over the lake: wind
looting the trees,
leaving paw-prints on the water
for the water-witch to read.

With the pass of a hand
it stops,
and the scoured lake
lies pewter-still
in a red, raking light, now
hardening to mirror.

Rinsed after the rain,
the forest is triggered and tripwired;
when I pause for a bird call
the silence takes time
to reassemble around me
like a dream retrieved.
No-one will find me here.

The ditches churn with frogs
and the track is lit
with their green and yellow
flattened stars.
Some let a cloudy scribble
milk out from their sides, like semen;
all of them carry the same rubric,
legible and bright.

The reed-pool trembles,
as if for a god.
Night switches through the trees.

In the open dark
all maps are useless:
the tracks are bloodied;
the tracks are washed clean.
Is this a way through the forest,
this path? Is this the way I came?

A SEAGULL MURMUR

is what they called it,
shaking their heads
like trawlermen;

the mewling sound of a leaking heart
    the sound
of a gull trapped in his chest.

To let it out
they ran a cut down his belly
like a fish, his open ribs

the ribs of a boat;
    and they closed him,
wired him shut.

Caulked and sea-worthy now
with his new valve; its metal
tapping away:

the dull clink
    of a signal-buoy
or a beak at the bars of a cage.

CALCUTTA, CO. ARMAGH

Like candy-striped
corner-store bags
caught in the trees
or snagged
in razor-wire,
washed-out
Union flags tatter
at every lamppost.

Outside the black fort,
April lays siege;
everything breaking out
in green: a green
straked through
with white bands of hawthorn
and the sharp, bright,
mustard-gold of gorse.

MAR-HAWK

Fed so long on washed meat and tirings
he is sharp-set, but fret-marked: hood-shy
and mantling; he bates at the perch,
won't come to the glove.

When we slip him on sprung quarry
he takes stand in the trees,
or rings up, towering, and rakes away,
unmade, unmanned.

THE CATCH

The tick you hear
is the heart-valve's catch,
holding back the wrong
traffic of blood;

this click is the notch in a run
of iron, and love is a ratchet
that slides only one way,
and cannot return.

ACTAEON: THE EARLY YEARS

A museum etiquette of table-mat and coaster,
ornaments that stayed put for decades: milkmaids,
donkeys, a weeping shepherdess and her china sheep;
it was a craft-shop Arcadia in a headache of pastels:
a shrine to hygiene and disappointment, a grief
he tiptoed through for years.

* * *

Her migraines were his fault, being the wrong child.
The best way, folk said, to be rid of changelings,
was to burn them with peat—send them hissing
up the chimney. The true child would be there by the fire
the next day. Not keeping turf, for the mess
it made, she used boiling milk, but it failed.

* * *

In his blue smock, sitting in a shambles
of coloured paper: 'You've ruined everything!'
she screamed, ruining everything.
The glue-bottle had a raw mouth
slit in its red rubber; he stabbed the table with it,
wanting to glue the world to bits.

* * *

A shore-dweller, he haunted the harled beach
with its broken toys, sucking boiled sweets
like sea glass. Once, after paddling,
he wanted to walk home nude

and fell—or was pushed—into a nettle-ditch.
She sewed him a suit of dock-leaves.

       *

His first death was on holiday, in a boy-sized
hole in the ground topped with corrugated iron
and brambles. He was dead all afternoon,
moist in the teeming dark, and had never been
so happy, alone there, untraceable. He hated
the hunger that brought him back to life.

       *

He stood waiting beside her as she talked
on the new telephone—a four-year-old
admiring her growing bulge. 'Look, Mummy,'
he said, 'now you have two bumps,'
meaning her breasts and her pregnancy.
She turned and knocked him to the floor.

       *

He learnt that desire for intimacy
was a transgression, and that
the resulting fear of intimacy,
which was also now a fear of disclosure,
was understandable, even natural,
in this place, among these people.

       *

The dunes were wired in a mesh of marram grass
and steel. The wind whittled the children thin and white
as they pleitered in the shallows with the dead crabs,

while the grown-ups shivered into their thermos flasks
behind wind-breaks and tank-traps,
shouting down to them to mind the dog-mess and the glass.

*

A man was standing over her, still dripping from the sea;
she looked up from the hand she was cradling in her lap,
to the boy in the doorway: her left thumb
pincushioned with the steel heads of dress-making pins
silvering the red meat. 'Pull them out,' said the swimmer
in the dream, 'every one, and your mother will be better.'

*

There was the comfort of sherbet fountains
and aniseed balls, foam bananas in wax-paper cones;
running home with a block of vanilla
wrapped in newspaper; the Sunday treat of a poke of chips
after seeing the grandparents. Best of all
the saved-up, sudden, consolation of chocolate.

*

He passed a slaughterhouse on the way to school:
a hall of cold columns, cream and red,
all turning slowly on their hooks.
He blessed himself: stunned at the passion, this
breaking-open, the rough grain of the blood sliding
between forefinger and thumb.

*

Some teachers customised the leather tawse they used
to beat the children's hands, frilling the end with a craft-knife.
'This is going to hurt me more than it will hurt you.'

On the pocket of his blazer, the school crest
was a pelican in her piety, feeding her young
with blood from her own breast.

*

You could smell the herring-catch come in each morning,
taste sea-salt on everything. Some folk swam
before they walked, they say, like his first girlfriend
with her lucken toes—said
to bring good fortune, show
that seal-blood sang in the veins.

*

From the top of the monkey puzzle, lit by the arced bow
of a new moon, he saw her, lying there in the bath: the white
face-mask first, then the rest. That hair. She must have
screamed as she covered her breasts because her face
chipped open, like her favourite porcelain fawn, the one
the cleaner broke. The hole at the muzzle like a smile, almost.

*

Hiding in the trees for hours was how he used to disappear:
that absence in the high-leafed branches, the canopy
opened to a sea of sky. Later, it was a well-shaft:
the tree inverted, sunk; he climbed down into its dark
and sat in the mulch of foliage, the black stars capsized,
his life capsized; his need to vanish, drowned.

*

When he left, he left no stain of himself on the paintwork's
magnolia, the carpets' analgesic-blue.
No sign or spoor. Twenty years spent

edging past a migraine's darkened room. He slipped a note into a gap in the floorboards:

'all the roads I walk will be away from you.'

TO MY DAUGHTERS, ASLEEP

Surrounded by trees I cannot name
that fill with birds I cannot tell apart

I see my children growing away from me;
the hinges of the heart are broken.

Is it too late to start, too late to learn
all the words for love before they wake?

FIRESETTING

Watching Italian TV all night
with the sound down:

                    in the aquarium light
rays dropping to the sea-floor in a flat
slap of dust,
each bomb-cloud lifting like a leisurely medusa;
the deep room bright with phosphor,
smoking ziggurats, back-lit,
and the tracer of trigger-fish across a city sky,
an after-image of morning.

SIESTA

after Montale

You lie through midday in the shade
of a sun-baked garden wall, pale,
absorbed by the crackle of blackbirds, the rustle
of snakes in the dry sticks and thorns;

you try to decipher the red lines of ants that scrawl
through the climbing plants, down through the ruts
of the scorched ground, to break and braid
and break again over the tops of their little mounds;

you might see, through the leaves, the distant pulse
of the sea, the distinct green scales of the waves,
while the churning of cicadas rises,
chiding and fricative, up from the empty heights.

And then you will walk, sun-blinded,
into the slow and bitter understanding
that all this life and all its heart-sick wonder
is just the following of a wall
ridged with bright shards of broken glass.

LA STANZA DELLE MOSCHE

The room sizzles in the morning sun;
a tinnitus of flies at the bright windows,
butting and dunting the glass. One dings
off the light, to the floor, vibrating blackly,
pittering against the wall before taxi
and take-off—another low moaning flight,
another fruitless stab at the world outside.
They drop on my desk, my hands,
and spin their long deaths on their backs
on the white tiles, first one way
then the other, tiny humming tops that
stop and start: a sputter of bad wiring,
whining to be stubbed out.

LIZARD

Volatile hybrid of dinosaur and toy, this
living remnant throbs on the hot stone:
a prehistoric offcut, six inches
of chlorophyll-green dusted with pollen;
a trick of nature—lithe, ectopic, cuneiform—
a stocking-filler, out of place everywhere
but in the sun. Frisking the wall,
its snatched run is a dotted line
of fits and starts, spasmodic, end-stopped.
It pulses once; slips into a rock with a gulp.

ODE TO CONGER-EEL BROTH

after Neruda

In Chile's
turbulent ocean
lives the rosy
conger,
a huge eel
with flesh
like snow.
And in Chilean pots
along the coast
the conger-eel broth
was born:
thick and rich,
a sea-gift
to mankind.
You bring the conger,
peeled,
to the kitchen,
its marbled skin slipped off
like a glove,
leaving this great
grape of the sea
exposed to the world;
naked,
the tender eel
glistens,
ready for us.
Now

you take some garlic,
slip out
the precious nub
of ivory,
smell
its dense aroma,
then
blend the crushed clove
with onion
and tomato
until the onion
turns to gold.
Meanwhile steam
our royal
Pacific prawns,
and when
they are
pink,
when the juices
of the ocean
and the clear liquid
released from the onion's light
bind together,
then
you introduce the eel
and let it slide into glory,
let it steep in the oils
of the pot, reduce
and marinate.
Now all that is needed
is a dollop of cream, dropped
into this heat

like an opening rose,
then to slowly simmer
until the essences of Chile
are warmed in the broth,
and the flavours
of land and sea
come to the table,
newly-married,
so that in this dish
you may understand heaven.

ASPARAGUS

Pushing up, hard and fibrous
from the ground, it is said to be
grown for the mouth:
steamed till supple
so the stem is still firm
but with a slight give to gravity.

Each wand has spurs
that swell in bedded layers
to the dark tip—slubbed and imbricate,
tight-set and over-lapping round the bud.
In a slather and slide, butter
floods at the bulb-head.

ON PHAROS

Four hollows and four seal-skins
on the beach, by a cave, their stink
undercut by the faint scent of ambrosia;
some tracks, of wild boar and panther;
the scales of a serpent; the hair,
perhaps, of a bearded lion;
torn leaves from a tree
when there were no trees anywhere near;
and, round a puddle of fresh water,
scorch-marks in the sand
and the signs of a struggle.
Seemed quiet enough now, though,
so we went and got our towels from the car.

MANIFEST

Try to reconstruct me from the heraldry of the flesh,
the thick blur of scar tissue, shreds of clothing,
that burst vessel in the eye like a twist in a marble,
those frost-feather wrinkles at the side of the mouth,
the sagittal crest, the arteries' complicated reds,
flakes of semen, the blonde hair at the nape of the neck
of either of my daughters, that cipher of birthmarks,
saliva on the whisky glass, the weight of the brain,
the weight of the heart, the bolus of the last meal,
the trace of morphine in the nails and in the grey hairs
of the chest, blood-string in the stool, gall-stones,
an ankle-spur, the retina's code, the death-mask,
life-mask, the bowel's gleet, the maze of fingerprints,
ruined teeth, signatures of taint and septicaemia,
the body's hieroglyphic marks, its flayed accoutrements,
this paraphernalia of clues; but you will never find me.
Shall I tell you? Shall I tell you the secret? *My whole life.*

UNTITLED (51)

for John Banville

Hello Hello Hello Hello
what shall we do today? Hello Today.

They come in procession: clown, princess,
scarecrow, ghost, a drift of the overgrown:
women in their institutional white socks
and black shoes, winter coats
over nighties, sheets, sack-dresses,
party hats, paper-bag masks
with eye-holes and straw,
hard plastic masks with white elastic:
cat, devil, crone.
They jostle, glitched and giggling,
holding hands, gripping their candy
and pocket-books, pennants and pinwheels.

I've got a boyfriend. He says I'm beautiful.
I told him you haven't seen the pretty parts.

A little hot under the masks, but liking
their new friends, the ghosts and devils,
these tranced angels
with the fixed faces and the moving eyes.

Haunted by everything but knowledge
—which is despair—they walk the field:
the masks and sheets and costumes
free them from themselves.

I want to run away from here
but I don't know how to run.

They gather acorns and beech-nuts
under the asylum trees, playing
Simon Says, running-on-the-spot.
They are innocent of the new one,
the one from outside, taking their pictures,
who saw the trees
crucified by camera-flash, the apples
browned to sweetbreads on the lawn.

Oh God, you're cute. You're too much.
Go ahead, dear. I'm sorry, I'm sorry.

This thin one, the visitor
with the huge green eyes,
lop-sided grin and squeaky voice,
pushes in amongst them:

What's wrong with her? a woman says,
pointing. *What's wrong with her?*

She stands at the back, with a half-smile,
as the shutter goes. Home at last.
She thinks what they are all thinking:
Am I the only one born?

NET

White silk
    in her hands
        across a crowded table,
the tumbled
    winter-drift
        of that
            unloosened scarf
drew me back
    to another ocean,
another ravishing.

    That moment,
        at twilight,
when a cloud
    of starlings
        slip-drags
            in a kite's tail
high over the remains of the pier,
    its undertow
        and backwash
trawling
    and spilling the net of itself,
to settle
    and lift
        from the dome
            like a black mantilla,
thrown and trailed and snatched away.

That moment,
            when I found myself
                        caught,
felt myself
            being pulled in.

CROSSING THE ARCHIPELAGO

Rising in November in these days of dusk
I am one life older, watching now as the walls
green over, the stones break into bud;
if this is ebb-tide turned to flood it means that
nightfall might begin again at dawn.
And so it does. The sea at Djurgården is a mirror
of lost light. I watch snowflakes fall on water,
transparent as tissue, melting back to nothing,
the black water's endless echo of the night.
A diminished life turns turtle and the day breaks
like a spell; to double back on this, through
ash and silver birch, to that extinguished past, a world
that's over, will wreck me. Hopeless to return
now: my future lit by bridges, and their burning.

BOW

A white dew
points the lawn;

I draw to full stretch,
blind-sighting in the dark

along the memory of your body.
Now there are no half-measures—

the flight is loosed, the flesh
invites the storm; I will

drive into your heart
up to the feathers.

RAINMAKER

Tentative rain, and the light
is changing, the water ticking
in the leaves, pattering the sheets
as she turns to him, murmuring
slow and ready for the verge of flood,
the undertow's hard covenant,
the run of trust.
She feels something unfurling
in a glut of dew, a finger pushing
into a peach, peach-water welling
over fern and fruit; she tastes the curve
and ache in the weather.
He unhooks her, and
leaning in
he starts to make her rain.

THE CUSTOM-HOUSE

after Montale

You don't remember the custom-house
or the drop to the rocks from its sheer height;
it's been waiting, lying empty since your grief
thickened to a swarm that night
and paused, trembling in the door.

For years, the south-westerlies have lashed
these ancient walls and now there is no love
left in your laugh: the compass spins,
free-wheeling; the dice are wrong.
You don't remember; other things distract you;
you are winding back the line onto the reel.

A strand is still anchored in me, but the house
drifts away; its weathervane, unhinged
and blackened, clatters round and round.
I hold a strand at anchor here
but you have gone, listing into your own dark.

On the lost horizon, the tankers kill their lights.
Is this the sea-route here, safe passage?
The waves still crash under the cliffs.
You don't remember the house, or this,
my famous evening, and I don't know now
who stays and who is leaving.

LEAVINGS

Still sleepwalking through her life,
I wrap her up
and we go through the snow that fell all night
and all through this Christmas morning:
her trainers barely denting the whitened lawn, her
two strides for every stride of mine.

Leaving her home
to the warmth of the house
I step back out, and see where my footprints turn
and walk through hers,
the other way—following the trail
of rabbit and deer into the unreachable silences of snow.
I can bring nothing of this back intact.
My face is smoke, my body water,
my tracks are made of snow.

The next morning is a dripping thaw, and winter
is gone from the grass—except for a line
of white marks going nowhere:
the stamped ellipses of impacted snow;
everything gone, leaving just this, this ghost-tread,
these wafer-thin footsteps of glass.

DONEGAL

for Ellie

Ardent on the beach at Rossnowlagh
on the last day of summer,
you ran through the shallows
throwing off shoes, and shirt and towel
like the seasons, the city's years,
all caught in my arms
as I ploughed on behind you, guardian still
of dry clothes, of this little heart
not quite thirteen,
breasting the waves
and calling back to me
to join you, swimming in the Atlantic
on the last day of summer.
I saw a man in the shallows
with his hands full of clothes, full of
all the years,
and his daughter going
where he knew he could not follow.

TRUMPETER SWAN

He takes a run at it: heaving himself
up off the lake, wing-beats echoing,
the wheeze of each pull
pulling him clear.

The sky is empty;
every stretch of water
flaunts its light.

You can learn how to fly, see all the edges
soften and blur, but you can't hold on
to the height you find,
you can never be taught how to fall.

ANSWERS

when mussels bud from every tree
when the fox lies down with the goose
when the sun and moon dance on the green
and oranges fruit in the bramble bush

when all streams run together
when all the streams stand still
when the cuckoo calls in winter
and water rolls back to the top of the hill

when herring swim the mountain lake
when their feathers sink like stars
when blackbirds fish the salt-sea wave
and the rabbit picks at the buzzard's heart

when seals come walking up from the bay
and nightfall begins with the morning dew
when daffodils open on Christmas Day and you see
a crow as white as a dove
I will return to you, my love, I will return to you

HOLDING PROTEUS

Becalmed here
on this salt beach far from home,
my boat blisters and flakes in the sun;
it has forgotten the sea
as I have forgotten the sea's purpose,
which is to change.
Sea-voyager, law-maker, warrior,
I walk in my own footprints now
around this island,
around myself, waiting for wind, trying
to hazard the heart's meridian,
a draught of air, a star to steer by.

My hands have been still for so long
they can't tell what they hold.

I've tried to buy the wind with coins
thrown from the water's edge, whistled
till my lips were raw, taken a whip
to the ship's boy, cut a pig's throat
with my own sword, sung
each of the supplicant songs,
untied all three magic knots in the cord
—no breeze, no wind, no storm.
The sea is deadpan.
I have worshipped the wrong gods.

I fall asleep over my book
of maps and legends, and I am char,
I am the fire-flags in the ashes of the field,
black-drowned in the marl-pit,
the unstrung heretic crouched in marram.
I am that rocking grief, those numb limbs.
I am the child, abandoned on the beach.

You turn, in my arms, to a deer,
a dolphin, shivering aspen, tiger, eel,
lithe root of flame and broken water.
I hold you fast, until you are flesh again,
seal-herder, seer, sea-guardian:
you who can only tell the truth,
show me how to find a fresh wind
and a safe harbour.

I wake to sea-storm, sunstorm, bright waves;
the sea-wind tearing pages from my book.

NOTES

Primavera

Some licence has been allowed with the phenological facts, but the poem is, in essence, accurate. If measured over flat ground, seasonal change moves at something close to walking speed. If global temperatures are allowed to increase at the current rate, in forty years Spring will arrive a fortnight earlier than it does today.

The Eel

'L'anguilla' from *La Bufera e Altro*

The Death of Actaeon

from *Metamorphoses*, Book III

Selkie

selkie: in Celtic legend, selkies are shape-changers with the ability to live in two elements; they swim as seals in the water but can cast off their pelts on land and assume human form.

bodhrán: (Irish) a traditional Irish drum; pronounced *bough-rawn*

Samhain

Samhain: (Irish) the first day of November; the festival of the dead, the beginning of the Celtic new year; pronounced *sow-in*

Strindberg in London

Strindberg visited London briefly, in 1893, on honeymoon with his second wife, Frida. He was unhappy, and left early.

snilleblixt: (Swedish) brainwave; flash of genius

Strindberg in Paris

Strindberg took a room in the Hôtel Orfila in early 1896, separated from his wife and children. He wrote *Inferno* here, and began his 'Occult Diary', devoting much time to chemistry, and particularly experiments in alchemy, which—along with depression and absinthe—exacerbated the severe psoriasis on his hands.

Entropy

hesitation-marks: preliminary, shallow slashes to the wrist

Sea-Fret

The prominent headland at Tynemouth in Northumberland was the site of an Anglian monastery before the Benedictine priory was established early in the 11th century. Because of the area's strategic importance, the monastic life co-existed with a military one, and the priory developed within a castle enclosure. These fortifications remained in use after the Dissolution, the coastal battery offering protection to the mouth of the Tyne during the wars against France and Germany. The guns were decommissioned in 1956.

Mar-Hawk

mar-hawk: a hawk that has been spoilt by clumsy handling

washed meat: meat soaked in water for a day then squeezed nearly white to deprive it of its natural juices and goodness; will keep the hawk's digestive organs in working order but reduce its condition (weight)

tirings: tough pieces of meat given to a hawk to pull at, in order to prolong the meal and exercise the muscles of the back and neck and sharpen the beak

sharp-set: keen and in hunting condition

fret-marks: traces or lines appearing across the webbing of feathers, caused by stress or hunger in immaturity; also known as 'hunger-traces'

hood-shy: a hawk that dislikes being hooded, generally through a fault of the falconer

to mantle: to stand over a kill with wings lowered and spread out to hide the food

to bate: to attempt to fly off the fist or perch when held or tied, in impatience or fright

to slip: to release a hawk at quarry

to spring: to flush the quarry

to take stand: to perch in a tree

to ring up: to climb in spirals

to tower: to soar up and hover

to rake away: to drift away too far while waiting-on (circling at a good height); giving up the flight

to make: to completely train a hawk, when he is said to be 'made'

to man: to tame a hawk by accustoming him to a man's presence

Actaeon: The Early Years

pleitered: (Scots) dabbled aimlessly with the hands and feet

lucken toes: (Scots) toes joined by a web of skin; those born with this condition were sometimes known as *Sliocha nan Ron*, the Children of the Seal

Siesta

'Merriggiare pallido e assorto' from *Ossi di Seppia*

La Stanza delle Mosche

La Stanza delle Mosche: (Italian) The Room of Flies

Ode to Conger-Eel Broth

'Oda al Caldillo de Congrio' from *Odas Elementales*

On Pharos and **Holding Proteus**

In Book IV of the *Odyssey*, Menelaus, King of Sparta, recalls being becalmed under the spell of the gods on the island of

Pharos. He meets Eidothea, who advises him to capture her father Proteus, the Old Man of the Sea: a prophet who so dislikes being questioned that he will assume any form to avoid his questioners. Menelaus and three companions lie in wait, covered in freshly flayed seal-skins, and surprise the sea-god on the beach. They hold him tight as he changes successively into a variety of animal, vegetable and elemental forms before returning to the human. Proteus is then obliged to break the binding spell and free the waters.

Untitled (51)

Between 1969 and 1971, Diane Arbus visited a number of 'retarded schools' in New Jersey, taking a series of photographs that would eventually be edited and published as *Untitled* (1995). The lines in italic are the recorded speech of some of the inmates, taken from Arbus's working notebooks and correspondence (*Revelations*, 2003).

The Custom-House

'La casa dei doganieri' from *Le Occasioni*

ACKNOWLEDGEMENTS

Acknowledgements are due to the editors of the following:

Guardian, London Review of Books, Los Angeles Review, New Republic, New York Review of Books, New Yorker, Poetry, Poetry London, Times Literary Supplement

'Actaeon: The Early Years' was published as a limited edition chapbook by Grand Phoenix Press (Nîmes, 2005); 'Primavera' was commissioned by John Burnside and Maurice Riordan for their anthology *Wild Reckoning* (Gulbenkian, 2004); 'Sea-Fret' was commissioned by Russell Mills and Ian Walton towards an installation called 'Static' for North Tyneside; 'Still Life with Cardoon and Carrots' was commissioned by Jo Shapcott for the 2002 *Poetry Proms* (BBC Radio 3).

I am grateful for time spent at the Santa Maddalena Foundation, Tuscany, the Tyrone Guthrie Centre at Annaghmakerrig, Co. Monaghan and in Trevilley, Cornwall.

My particular thanks to James Lasdun and Don Paterson for their advice and close reading.